What's in this book

This book belongs to

T0351531

_____

我们和大自然
Nature and us

学习内容 Contents

沟通 Communication

说说自然景物
Talk about mother nature

背景介绍：
小朋友们在不同季节里享受大自然。

生词 New words

★	天	sky
★	地	land
★	云	cloud
★	山	mountain
★	海	sea
★	花	flower
★	草	grass
★	小	small
★	真	really

树	tree
石头	rock
冷	cold
热	hot
大自然	nature

句式 Sentence patterns

天真高，海真大。

The sky and the sea are really big.

跨学科学习 Project

在地图上标示地点，并认识方位

Mark places on the map and learn about their positions

文化 Cultures

中国风景景观

Scenic landscapes in China

Get ready

1 Do you like to be close to nature?

2 What do you see in the countryside?

3 Do you prefer hiking or going to the beach?

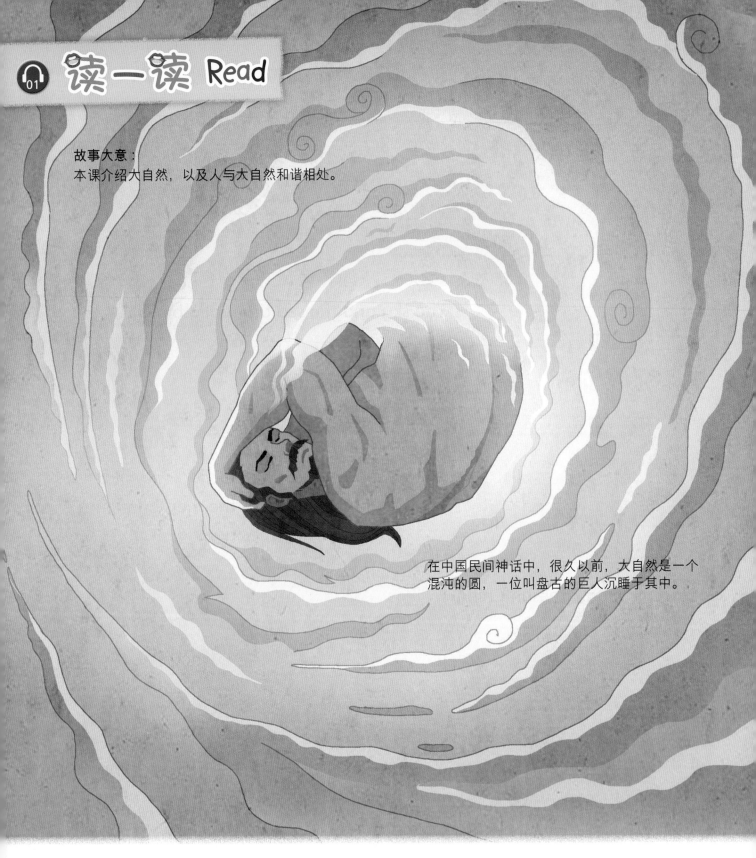

故事大意：
本课介绍大自然，以及人与大自然和谐相处。

在中国民间神话中，很久以前，大自然是一个混沌的圆，一位叫盘古的巨人沉睡于其中。

大自然是一个很大很大的圆。

参考问题和答案：

1 What does nature look like? (Nature looks like a huge circle.)

2 There is a man in the circle. Do you think he is real or a fictional figure?
(He is a fictional figure./I do not know.)

tiān

天

dì

地

后来，盘古醒了，他用斧头将大自然分开，上面是天，下面是地。盘古怕它们还会合在一起，就努力用手撑天，用脚瞪地。最后，盘古累倒了，他的身体逐渐变成了大自然中的万物。

参考问题和答案：

1 What did the man do with the axe? (He used the axe to separate nature into two.)
2 What is he doing? (He is using his arm and legs to prevent the sky above and the land below from coming together.)

一天，圆分开了，上面是天，下面是地。

提醒学生本课结合神话故事和真实景物，图中的景象是透过盘古的角度来阐述的。

yún
云

shān
山

shí tou
石头

天上有云，地上有山和石头。

参考问题和答案：

1 What are the white things in the sky? (They are clouds.)
2 What are the huge green things on the land? (They are mountains.)
3 What are the small grey things on the land? (They are rocks.)

参考问题和答案:

1　What is under the mountains? (It is the sea.)
2　How does the seawater feel? And how about the land? (The seawater is cold and the land is hot.)

hǎi
海

lěng
冷

rè
热

"冷"和"热"是一对反义词。

山下面是海。海水很冷，地面很热。

海边的日夜温差比沙地要小得多，主要是因为水的温度变化比沙小。因此，相同日照下，海水温度比沙地温度低。

shù
树

huā
花

cǎo
草

参考问题和答案：

1 What are the tall plants on the land? (Those are trees.)
2 What are the short green plants on the land? (That is grass.)
3 What are the colourful and tiny plants? (Those are flowers.)

地上高的是树，矮的是花，小的是草。

xiǎo
小

dà   zì   rán
大 自 然

参考问题和答案：

1   Compared with nature, how do the human beings look? (They look very small and a part of nature.)
2   Do you think nature is marvellous? (Yes, I think so. Nature is beautiful and wonderful.)

地上还有小小的人。
大自然真奇妙！

Let's think

1 ## Circle six natural objects mentioned in the story.

先让学生回忆第4至9页中出现的自然景物名称，再圈出图中的景物。

云　　天
山
树　　海
石头

2 ## Look at the pictures. Tick the ones that you like. Tell your friend the reasons.

参考表述：
I like the green forest because the earth is healthy./I like the blue ocean because it is clean and beautiful.

学生讨论完后，老师总结：我们要爱护大自然的一草一木，不能破坏大自然的生态平衡。
人与自然应该和谐共处。

New words

02

1 Learn the new words.

延伸活动：
学生两人一组，一人随机说出生词，另一人指出图中相应的事物，
反之亦可。

天　大自然　云　山　树　真热。　海　真冷。　石头　地　草　花　小

2 Match the words to the pictures. Write the letters.

a 云　　b 海　　c 花　　d 山　　e 石头　　f 草

b

a

e

c

f

d

听听说说 Listen and say

03 **1** Listen and circle the correct answers.

04 **2** Look at the pictures. Listen to the st

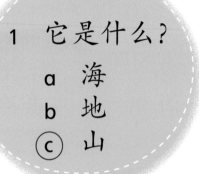

1 它是什么？
a 海
b 地
ⓒ 山

2 它是什么？
a 天
ⓑ 云
c 花

3 它是什么？
a 草
ⓑ 花
c 树

1 这是什么？

上面是天，下面是地。

3 地上也有树、花、草、石头。

第二题参考问题和答案：

What objects in nature do you like most? Why?
(I like clouds. The clouds have various shapes and
are like cotton candy./I love flowers because of
their colours and good smell.)

d say.

4

3 Talk about the pictures
with your friend.

学生两人一组，互相问答。鼓励学生回答时尽量用上修饰的词语，如"我看见高高的山。""我看见蓝蓝的天上有白色的云。"

你看见什么？

我看见……

Task

先让学生完成日志，其中前三题尽量用汉字书写，后面一题则在合适的项目上打钩。然后进行讨论，建议句式"我喜欢/看见……""……很……"等。

Recall a field trip you went on and complete the journal. Talk about it with your friend.

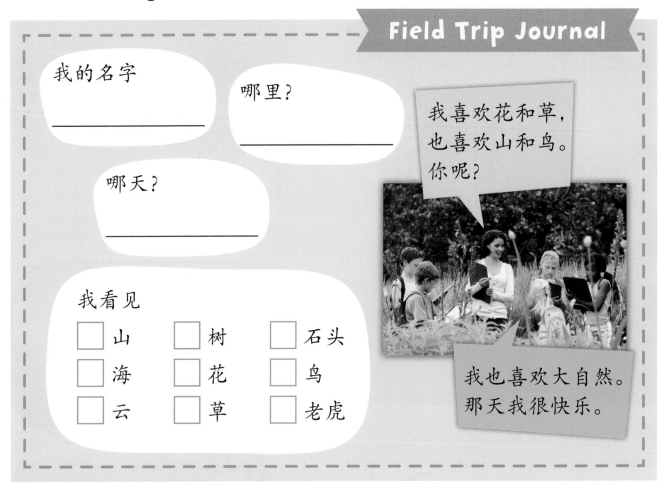

Field Trip Journal

我的名字

_____

哪里？

_____

哪天？

_____

我看见

☐ 山 ☐ 树 ☐ 石头
☐ 海 ☐ 花 ☐ 鸟
☐ 云 ☐ 草 ☐ 老虎

我喜欢花和草，也喜欢山和鸟。你呢？

我也喜欢大自然。那天我很快乐。

Game

Help the caterpillar get to the grass and talk to the frog. Circle 鱼 in the pond.

老师提醒学生，在走迷宫时，除了顺利到达出口见到青蛙，还要尽可能经过所有的草地。

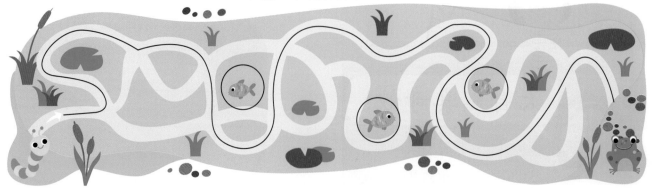

Song

🎧 **05** **Listen and sing.**

学生一边唱歌，一边配合歌词指认图上的景物。

大自然真大。

天上有云，

云下有山，

山下有海，

海旁有地。

地上有石头，

有树、花和草，

还有小小的我们。

课堂用语 Classroom language

用一用？

"我可以……吗？"用来礼貌地询问是否可以做某事。

我可以去厕所吗？
May I go to the washroom, please?

我可以用一用吗？
May I use it, please?

15

写一写 Write

1 Review and trace the strokes. 提醒学生先回忆笔画名称及其写法，再进行描写。

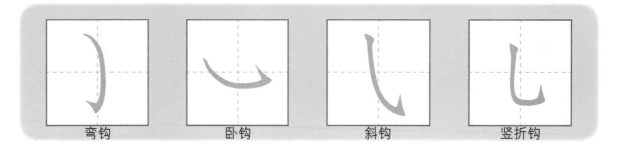

弯钩　　　　卧钩　　　　斜钩　　　　竖折钩

2 Learn the component. Trace ⺿ to complete the characters.

花　苗　茶　菇

学生描完后老师做总结："草字头"多表示一些草本植物。

3 Colour ⺿ for fruits red, for vegetables green and for flowers orange.

香蕉

菇　绿色

葡萄　红色

茄子　绿色

苹果　红色

菊花　橙色

茶花　橙色

4 Trace and write the characters.

花

一 十 艹 艹 艻 花 花

花	花		

草

一 十 艹 艹 芍 苩 苩 莒 草

草	草		

5 Write and say.

绿色的是树和 草 ，红

色、黄色、白色的是 花 。

汉字小常识 Did you know?

Colour the characters in any colour you like. 这些字的结构是镶嵌结构。

In some characters, several components merge with one another to form a single structure.

果	来	夹	爽	夷

多元学习 Connections

Cultures

中国地域辽阔，自然风光独具特色。老师可以简单介绍图片中的地方，再由学生根据图片中的景色自由发言。建议句式"我喜欢……""……很/真……""这里有……""这些是……"

China is a big country with spectacular landscapes. Look at the pictures and talk about these places with your friend.

Guangxi　广西 桂林山水

这里的山和水真好看。

Shandong　山东 泰山日出

我喜欢看云。

云南 石林　Yunnan

这些是山还是石头？

Inner Mongolia　内蒙古 大草原

天真蓝，草地真绿。

Zhejiang　浙江 杭州西湖

花很好看。

香港 维多利亚港　Hong Kong

这里有山有海。

1 Work with your friend. Match the pictures to the correct words. Then tell your friend which picture you like the most and why.

冷 ___c, d___

热 ___a, b___

高山 ___d___

大海 ___b___

大树 ___c___

草地 ___a___

2 Draw a scenic place and tell your friend why it is a good place to visit.

温习 Checkpoint

学生4至5人一组，先填写句子中的空缺，然后以做报告的形式向小组同学讲说。在完成活动的过程中，简单认识香港的一些旅游点。

1 Help Hao Hao finish his travel scrapbook so he can tell his friends about his holiday.

我在天上。天真高，海真大。

十月，不冷也不热。

它在哪里？它在 山 上。

蓝色的 天 ，白色的云，很好看。

树上有小小的 花 。

我喜欢大自然，山上有树和 草 ，山下有海和小石头。

评核方法：
学生两人一组，互相考察评价表内单词和句子的听说读写。交际沟通部分由老师朗读要求，学生再互相对话。
如果达到了某项技能要求，则用色笔将星星或小辣椒涂色。

2 Work with your friend. Colour the stars and the chillies.

Words	说	读	写
天	☆	☆	🌶
地	☆	☆	🌶
云	☆	☆	🌶
山	☆	☆	☆
海	☆	☆	🌶
花	☆	☆	☆
草	☆	☆	☆
小	☆	☆	🌶
真	☆	☆	🌶
树	☆	🌶	🌶
石头	☆	🌶	🌶

Words and sentences	说	读	写
冷	☆	🌶	🌶
热	☆	🌶	🌶
大自然	☆	🌶	🌶
蓝色的天，白色的云。	☆	🌶	🌶
天真高，海真大。	☆	🌶	🌶
Talk about mother nature	☆		

3 What does your teacher say?

评核建议：
根据学生课堂表现，分别给予"太棒了！
(Excellent!)"、"不错！(Good!)"或"继续努
力！(Work harder!)"的评价，再让学生圈出
上方对应的表情，以记录自己的学习情况。

My teacher says ...

分享 Sharing

Words I remember

天	tiān	sky
地	dì	land
云	yún	cloud
山	shān	mountain
海	hǎi	sea
花	huā	flower
草	cǎo	grass
小	xiǎo	small
真	zhēn	really
树	shù	tree
石头	shí tou	rock

冷	lěng	cold
热	rè	hot
大自然	dà zì rán	nature

延伸活动：

1 学生用手遮盖英文，读中文单词，并思考单词意思；
2 学生用手遮盖中文单词，看着英文说出对应的中文单词；
3 学生两人一组，尽量运用中文单词复述第4至9页内容。

Other words

分开	fēn kāi	to separate
海水	hǎi shuǐ	sea water
地面	dì miàn	ground
还有	hái yǒu	also
奇妙	qí miào	wonderful

OXFORD
UNIVERSITY PRESS

Oxford University Press is a department of the University of Oxford.
It furthers the University's objective of excellence in research, scholarship,
and education by publishing worldwide. Oxford is a registered trade mark of
Oxford University Press in the UK and in certain other countries

Published in Hong Kong by
Oxford University Press (China) Limited
39th Floor, One Kowloon, 1 Wang Yuen Street, Kowloon Bay,
Hong Kong

© Oxford University Press (China) Limited 2017

The moral rights of the author have been asserted

First Edition published in 2017

Illustrated by Anne Lee, KK Ng, KY Chan and Wildman

Photographs for reproduction permitted by Dreamstime.com

China National Publications Import & Export (Group) Corporation is an authorized distributor of
Oxford Elementary Chinese.

Please contact content@cnpiec.com.cn or 86-10-65856782

ISBN: 978-0-19-082202-6

10 9 8 7 6 5 4 3 2

Teacher's Edition
ISBN: 978-0-19-082214-9

10 9 8 7 6 5 4 3 2